BECAUSE OF YOUR faith IT WILL happen

– MATTHEW 9:29B –

This Book
Belongs To

_____

Because you know that

the testing of your f...

Bible Verse about F...

NOTHING

WHILE

...ES

...ILY

ISBN : 978-1530381227

Dream Catcher Coloring Book   ISBN : 978-1546311560

Free Download Coloring Pages

At : bit.ly/get_sample_free

Let us hold fast the confession of our hope without wavering, for he who promised is faithful

Hebrews 10:23

Arise, for it is your task, and we are with you; be strong and do it

Ezra 10:4

Look to the LORD and his strength; seek his face always

Chronicles 16:11

Jesus Christ **is** the same yesterday, **today,** and **forever**

Hebrews 13:8

YOU SHALL HAVE NO OTHER GODS BEFORE ME

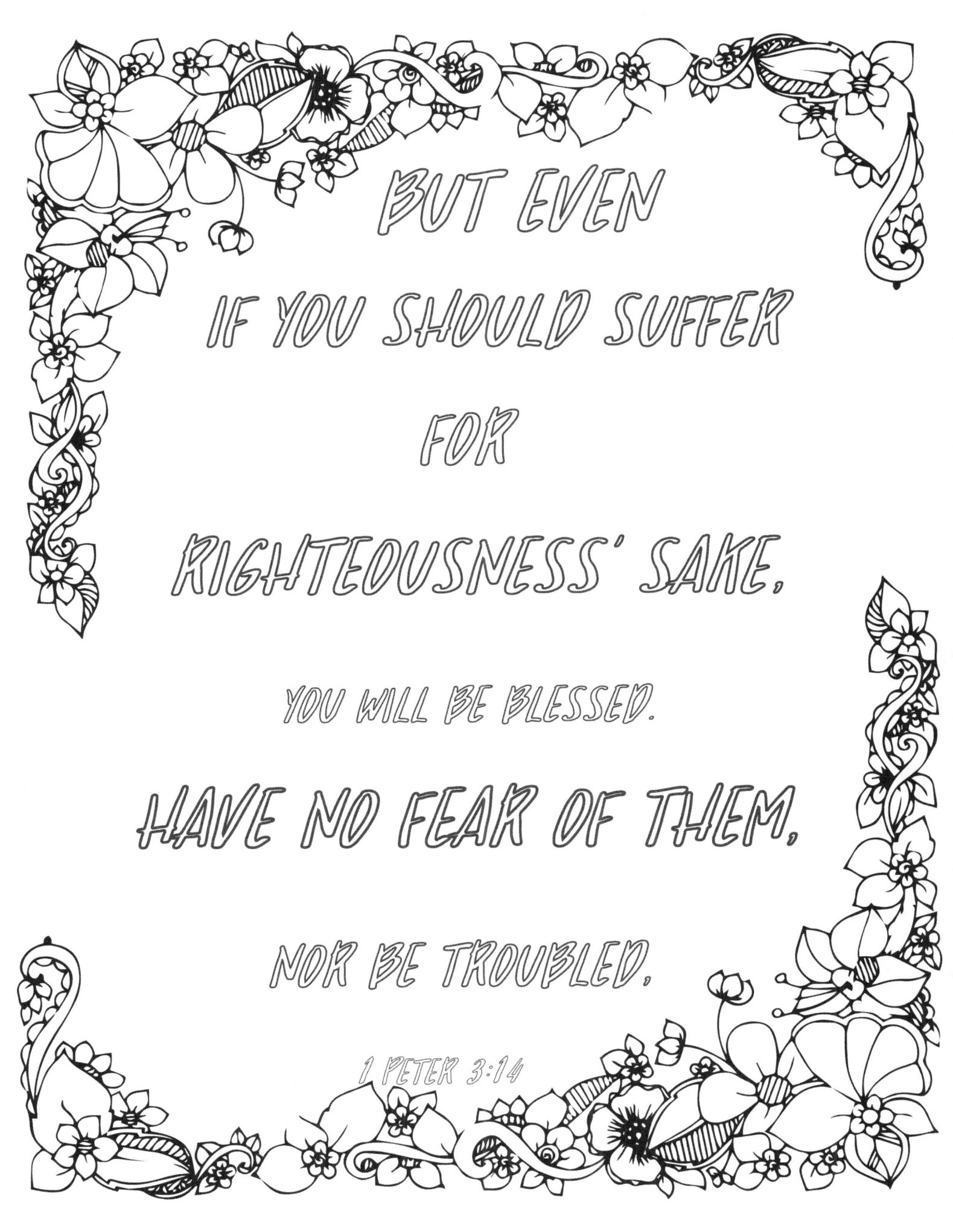

BUT EVEN
IF YOU SHOULD SUFFER
FOR
RIGHTEOUSNESS' SAKE,

YOU WILL BE BLESSED.

HAVE NO FEAR OF THEM,

NOR BE TROUBLED.

1 PETER 3:14

for I know the plans I have for you, declares the LORD, plans for welfare and not for evil, to give you a future and a hope.

Jeremiah 29:11

I have hidden your word in my heart that I might not sin against you

Psalm 119:11

The Lord is my light and my salvation whom shall I fear?

Psalm 27:1

for all
have sinned
fall short of
the glory
of God,

Romans 3:23

But godliness with contentment is great gain

Timothy 6:6

This is the day
that
the LORD
has made;
let us rejoice   and
be glad in it

Psalms 118:24

For all have sinned and fall short of the glory of God

Romans 3:23

I am with you always

Matthew 28:20

Everyone who calls on the name of the Lord will be saved

The Lord is good to all

Psalm 145:9

Be kind to one another

Ephesians 4:32

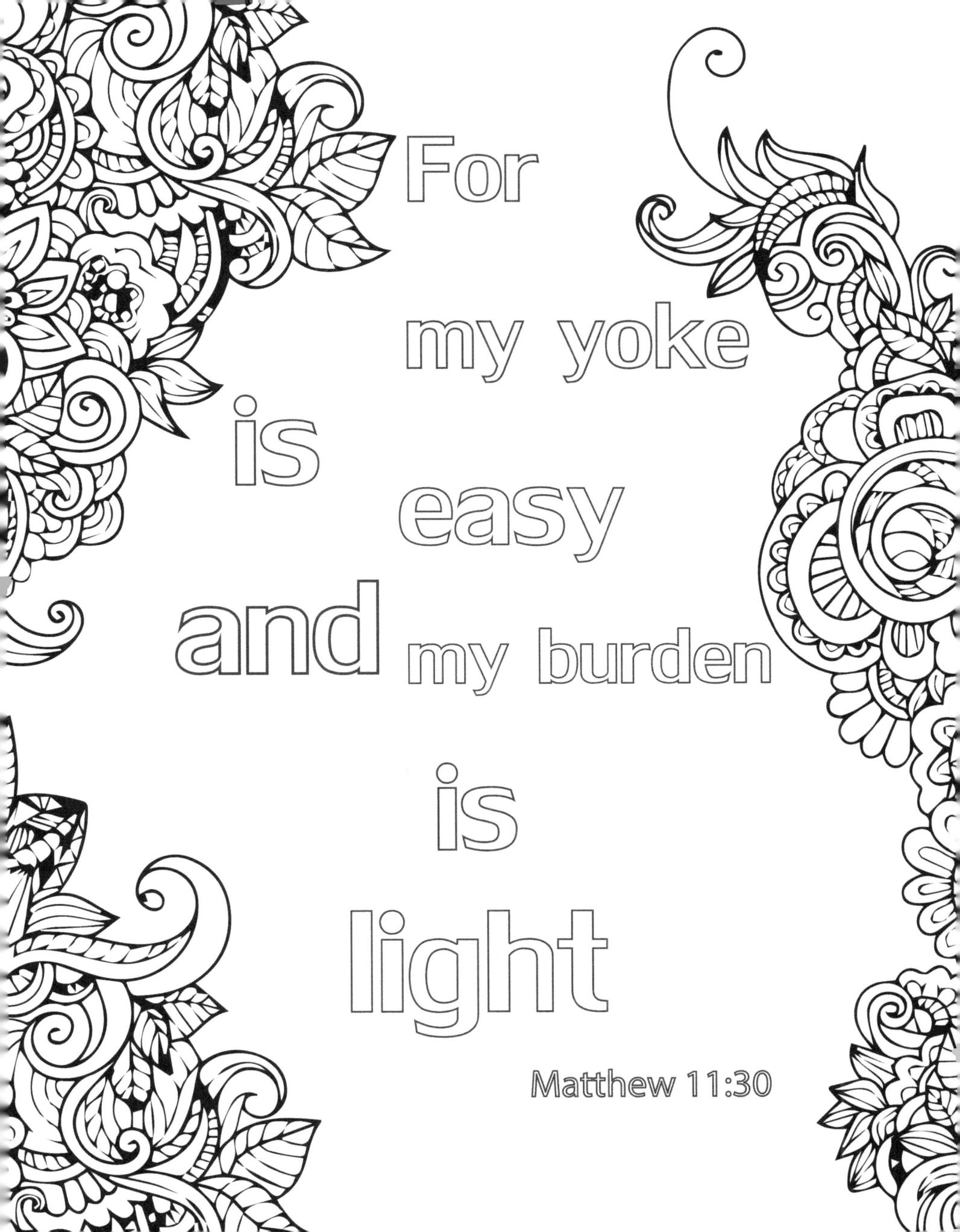

For my yoke is easy and my burden is light

Matthew 11:30

Therefore submit to God. Resist the devil and he will flee from you

James 4:7

Love

one

another

1 John 3:23

You are the light of the world

CHILDREN,

OBEY

YOUR PARENTS

IN ALL THINGS

COLOSSIANS 3:20

Every good gift and every perfect gift is from above

James 1:17

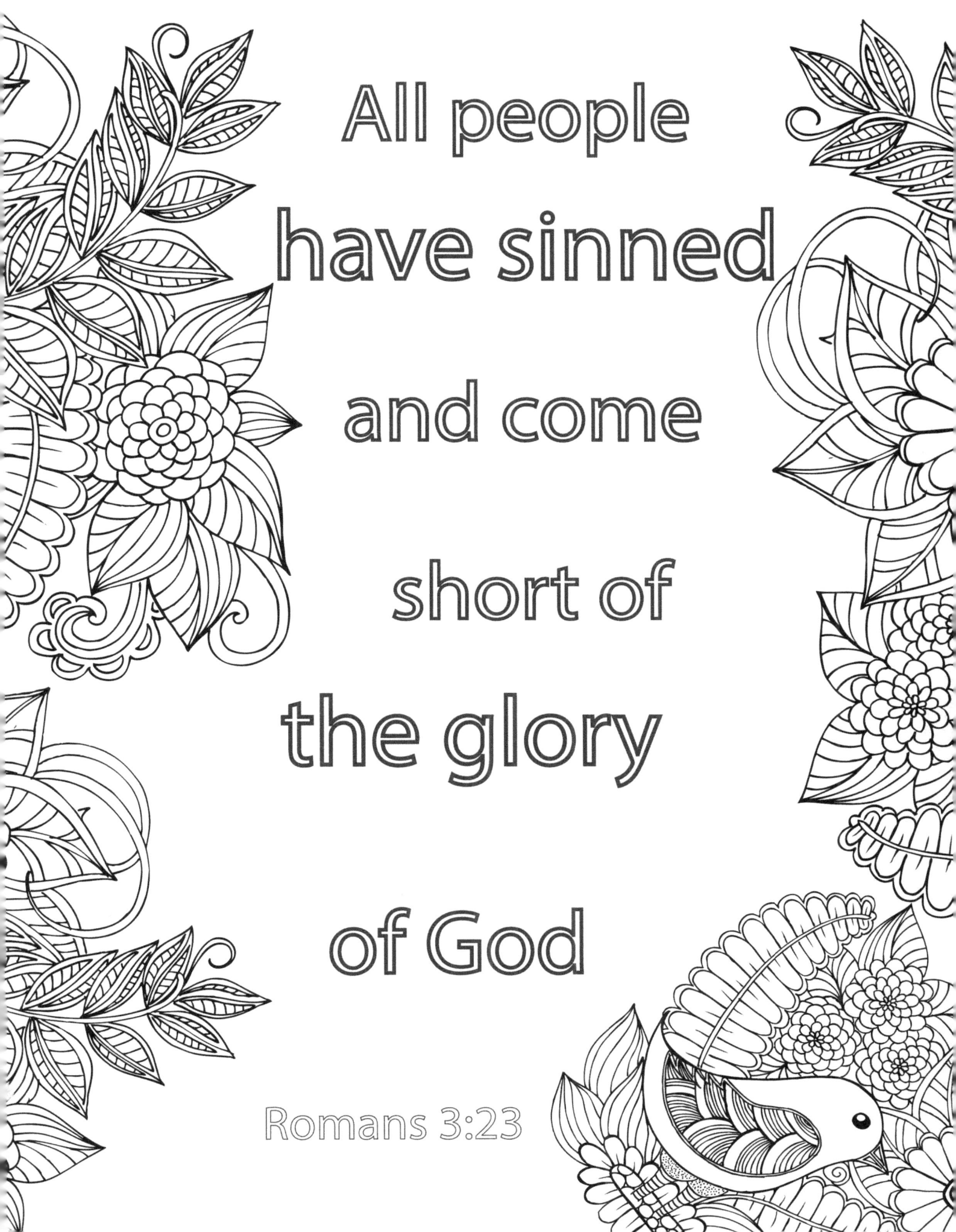

All people have sinned and come short of the glory of God

Romans 3:23

www.ingramcontent.com/pod-product-compliance
Lightning Source LLC
Chambersburg PA
CBHW081152280526
45787CB00008B/3304